WHAT'S **YOUR** SUPERPOWER?

WHAT'S **YOUR** SUPERPOWER?

From Special Needs to Super Heroes

MARCY VALENZUELA

www.WhatsYourSuperpowerBooks.com

IC PRESS

Idea Creations Press
www.ideacreationspress.com

IC
PRESS
Idea Creations Press
www.ideacreationspress.com

978-1-948804-09-7

Publisher's Catalog-In-Publishing Data

Valenzuela, Marcy author
What's YOUR Superpower? / Marcy Valenzuela
First trade paperback original edition. | Salt Lake City: Idea Creations Press, 2020.
ISBN 978-1-948804-09-7 | LCCN 2018963780
Inspirational Children. | BISAC: RELIGION / Inspirational | SELF-HELP / Spiritual

Cover art and interior illustrations by Robinson Valenzuela
www.RobinsonValenzuela.com
Designed by Douglas Jones

www.WhatsYourSuperpowerBooks.com

Printed in the U. S. A

This book is dedicated to:

All people with unique super powers, both friends and angels.

All the orphans around the world. Your voice is being heard, your parents are coming.

Special heart-felt thank you to the families and individuals who made it possible for this book to become a reality.

In loving memory of

Ryker Bryce Peterson
March 6, 2004 – February 10, 2018

&

Jeffery Roy Hasara
November 23, 1993 – August 16, 2010

Table of Contents

Sofia & Ariana

Ariana & Sofia

WHAT'S YOUR SUPERPOWER?

"We love to hug everyone and give the best loves and hugs in the whole world."

Hi, I'm Ariana. This is my sister, Sofia. She grew up in an orphanage. When she was three years old our family adopted her from Armenia. We love to eat pizza and play at the park. Swings and slides are our favorite. When we hear music, it makes us happy and we dance all over the house. I'm always in a dress and like to be a pretty little lady. Sofi likes to jump on beds, chairs, off furniture; everything. We love jumping so much that we have two trampolines. We have a little one inside and a big trampoline outside that we take turns on with our brother, Duke. We often get mistaken for twins, and when we all ride in the shopping cart people think we're triplets.

We love adventures and learning more about our world. In our kitchen, Mama puts locks on the bottom cupboards and the top ones too. That's where her vitamins and cookies go. We spilled them in the sink one day and got in big trouble. The next day we went to explore but we couldn't open it!

It takes us two to three times longer to learn things compared to other kids our age. Mama repeats things a lot, and we like it when she sings songs, that's our favorite way of learning new things, like ABC's, shapes, colors, the potty song and all of the funny songs Mama makes up to make us laugh and learn. You should hear OUR version of *Pat-a-Cake* and *Itsy-Bitsy Spider*.

We are learning to read and love story books. Mama puts word strips around the house on different things, like the fridge, mirror, piano, potty, and bed. We are learning by word recognition and association, not phonics, not yet anyway. We're still learning our letter sounds. We like to do a lot of matching with pictures and word strips, that's a fun game.

Sofi can make letter sounds a little better than me. I have a mild hearing loss in my ears and use a Baha hearing aid. It's attached to an elastic headband and they rest on the bone behind my ears, sending sound through the bones in my head directly into my hearing nerve.

We are as bendable as gymnasts and can easily put our feet over our head. Sofi will randomly be standing and stick one leg straight up in the air like she's about to give a high five with her foot. We love Equine therapy and ride our neighbor's horse, Tav. It helps our muscles in our middle and our legs get stronger and help us balance, run, and stand up without falling.

Sofi is a little more outgoing than I am. She's always making friends and climbing on Mommy's friends for a hug. I'm a little shyer. It takes me a while to get comfortable around new people. I'm happy to play by myself with my Barbies and dollhouse. Sofi prefers playing with someone like brother, Duke, or throwing the ball for our black lab. She's always laughing and it makes me laugh too. We're best friends.

When I was born Mama and Papa didn't know I had a little something extra. They didn't find out until I was four months old that my 21st chromosome had three copies. It's called Trisomy 21. Most people only have two.

My sister and I use sign language sometimes because it's hard to talk clearly. We love watching *Signing Time* and *Tree Schoolers* shows and have learned a lot of signs. When Sofi came home, she easily and quickly transitioned from Armenian to English. She learned English and sign language by watching and practicing *Signing Time* shows. Sometimes people can't understand what we are trying to say at all, but sign language bridges the gap for us. It makes us feel good being able to communicate even though we can't talk very well.

Sofi has a unique trait, a straight line across the palm of her left hand, but not her right hand. It's called a simian line. Lots of people with DS have this, but I don't. I have two lines on both hands like my brother. Both Sofi and I have curved pinkies that bend inward. The bones grew that way, it's called Clinodactyly. It doesn't hurt. Older people have had surgery to fix it, but not us.

I like to eat soft foods, it's too hard to eat apples or carrots, but I like chips and pretzels. Mama keeps trying to get me to eat new healthy food. She sneaks vitamins into my applesauce and it turns green.

Sofia was born with a little hole in her heart. She's six years old and the doctors said her heart is all better now. We have other friends like us that had to get open heart surgery to fix their heart. We remember when our friend Molly would get really tired just trying to eat because her heart was working so fast. We're glad our friend felt a lot better after her surgery and could run and play with us.

We grind our teeth when we're bored because we like the sound. It stimulates nerves in our head. The dentist said it's making our teeth small though. At night, mouth guards help our teeth get straight and help us not grind them when we sleep.

Sometimes Sofi will hit her head with her hand. She doesn't know how to express herself any other way. It's usually when she's upset or disappointed, like if I took the toy she was playing with.

I'm a great helper and help sister get her socks, shoes, and jacket on before school. I still get my shoes on the wrong feet, by mistake though. Sister Sofi loves tickles. Especially soft tickles under her chin and arm. She's like a kitty sometimes, going to Mama to get a chin tickle.

We are very aware of other people's feelings. Sofi is nearly always the first to give kisses for *owies* and say sorry when a mistake has been made. If you were to ask our family, they would tell you we are two of the most tender-hearted, loving, spunky little ladies you'll ever meet. We love to hug everyone and give the best loves and hugs in the whole world.

WE ARE ARIANA & SOFIA.
We have DOWN SYNDROME.
What's YOUR Superpower?

Josh and Rhett

Josh

WHAT'S YOUR SUPERPOWER?

Some people are surprised at my job. If you close one eye and look through a straw with your other eye, you'll understand why."

Hi, I'm Josh, I was born in Louisiana. I like reading books and cooking. One of my favorite foods to make is jambalaya and key lime pie. When I make cookies, I feel the edges to check when they are done. I love to listen to music and can closely mimic the voices of my favorite singers. My mother used to listen to Neal Diamond when I was a child. I've heard it so much I can sound exactly like him. I'll sing a little if my friends ask me to a party. People are always so surprised how close I sound like the real thing. I like making people happy and laugh.

One of my favorite video games is the classic Super Mario Brothers. Good ol' Nintendo. I have to sit very close to the TV. I can't read print effectively unless it's really large. And when I do read, it's only from my right eye.

I have a unique talent. When I think of numbers, I can see colors. Every number has a different color. When I was learning my numbers as a child, I would associate them with a color. All colors repeat as different shades in higher numbers.

1 - Black	2 - Gray	3 - Orange
4 - Blue	5 - Red	6 - Brown
7 - Tan/Orange	8 - Medium Orange	9 - Light Blue
10 - Dark Brown	11 - Dark Orange	12 - Bright Orange
13 - Yellow Orange	14 - Medium Blue	15 - Green
16 - Light Brown	17 - Light Orange Brown	18 - Light Orange
19 - Very Light Blue	20 - White	21 - White and Black

My favorite color is green. Anything green is a wonderful thing. Can you guess my favorite number?

I like computers so much that I became a software developer. Some people are surprised at my job. If you close one eye and look through a straw with your other eye, you'll understand why. I use a regular keyboard and a desktop or laptop when I work. Some people own fancy Braille keyboards, but I don't need that. I'm satisfied with what I have. I use what little vision I do have to see color and motion every day, even though I can't see a lot of detail.

I'm now 39 and have owned my own home for many years. I enjoy my independence, just like my older brother, Rhett, who is 41. We both work with computers and live in our own houses. Rhett is a Braille proof-reader of school books for the deaf and blind school. We both have an eye condition called Staphyloma. We were born with underdeveloped eyes. It has never gotten any worse than when we were born, but it also hasn't gotten any better.

I use public transportation to get where I need to go. I don't drive. To read email, or to receive other written information, I rely on electronic speech the majority of the time. I have a special program on my computer that is constantly talking to me, telling me what is displayed on the screen. At other times I read Braille with my fingers.

Some pop machines have Braille on the buttons, others have a touch-screen. When I use these machines, I need someone to help me get what I want. I typically don't use touch screens. They are not useful to me unless they are a special type that can read aloud... similar to my computer talking to me.

I walk with a white cane to feel the floor so I don't trip and know what's around me. I'm not much of a traveler, and weather in different seasons can be a challenge when I do travel. In the snow, the ground has a consistent, slick texture and I can't feel where things are with my feet or my white stick.

The world was designed for people who have sight. That doesn't stop me though. I make friends easily and am a great listener. My friends tell me they feel comfortable and accepted around me. I'm very social and love to visit with friends. Making people laugh is one of my favorite things to do. I make it a point to message my friends on their birthdays and give them a cheerful birthday wish. I think it's important for people to feel like they are remembered and matter. It's one way I show them I care.

MY NAME IS JOSH ⠠⠚⠕⠎⠓ (Josh)

I am BLIND ⠠⠃⠇ (blind)

What's YOUR Superpower?

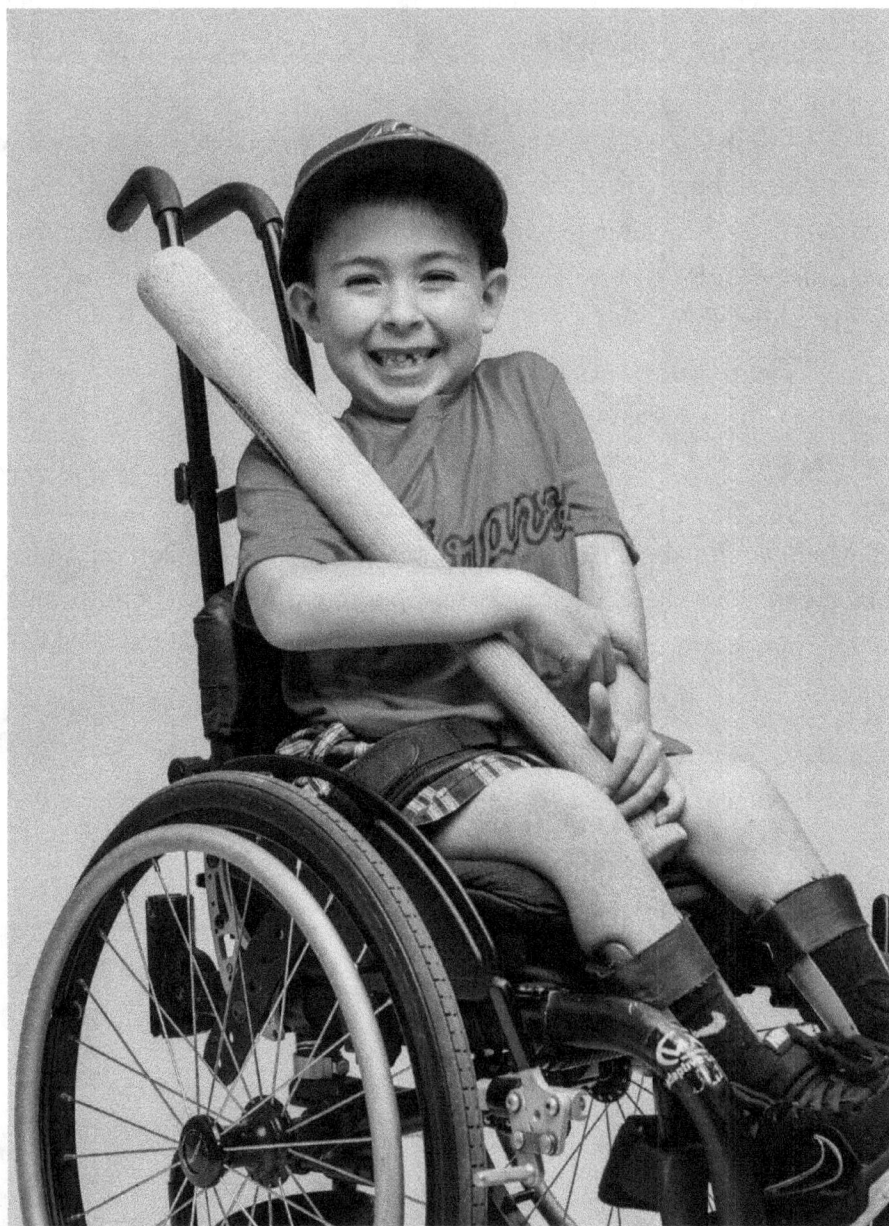

Adrian

WHAT'S YOUR SUPERPOWER?

"Whenever I'm in a crowd I'm always looking to find someone to make them smile."

Hi, I'm Adrian. I play baseball and ski, but I do it a little differently than most kids because I do it without using my legs! When I play inside, I like to draw. Some of my favorite pictures are of dinosaurs. I like playing video games on my PS4. Jurassic World and the Lego games are my favorite because they're just fun!

I'm super creative and like to build different worlds with my Legos, like on Minecraft. My greatest ambition is to be a paleontologist. I LOVE dinosaurs! I like them because they are large and can walk on all four legs. I like how each one has something that makes them mighty. My favorite are the raptors because they are super smart.

I want to become a scientist so I can bring dinosaurs back to life. I've written many stories about what the dinosaurs would do once I brought them to life. I want to create a dinosaur park and I already have a business plan written up! I first thought of that idea when I was only six years old.

I'm an actor and a model. I'm also a representative, or an ambassador, for Shriners Hospital. My favorite vacation was to Hawaii.

It's warm and reminds me of Jurassic World. I would love to live on Kauai one day.

When I was seven, I wanted a really cool Lego set but didn't have the money for it. I attended the *Kids Entrepreneurial Fair* where I created and sold garden signs and decorations. It was similar to décor you see for a fairy garden; but mine were for a dinosaur garden. I made a cost analysis and paid back the money I borrowed that I needed to make my products. I made $100 and was able to get the toy I wanted!

When I was born, my hip was dislocated and I was paralyzed from the knees down. I have no feeling below my knees and I can't walk. I use a wheelchair. I have ankle-foot orthotics or AFO braces that I wear to stabilize my legs. With my braces on, I use crutches. With my special tools, I can walk.

I have what's nicknamed the *Snowflake* disorder because everyone who has my same condition is completely different. Some of us can stand with crutches, but can't walk. Some can walk. Others use a manual or motorized wheelchair. Some have more ability to move than others who rely on someone else for assistance.

I don't go potty like most people. I have two ports or covered openings in my tummy that doctors made to help my body get rid of my potty. I spend two hours every night getting my tummy ports flushed, or pushed out with a saline/glycerin mixture. Nobody can see these though.

I had a malformation of thick bone by my brain stem when I was born that had to be shaved down. It's called a Chiari Malformation. It's because of this that I have sleep apnea and breathing problems. When I sleep at night I don't breathe very well. Sometimes I stop breathing, then wake up gasping for air. This is sleep apnea. At night I wear an oxygen tube that gives me fresh air in my nose so my body can breathe better as I sleep.

The question I get asked most often is: "What's that tube in your head?" I get asked about it all the time. You wanna know why?

When I was born, I had a little water sack that built up with spinal fluid on my lower back. Parts of my backbone were not connected when I was born, L4 and L5. I had surgery when I was only a few days old to fix this and close the gap. Now that the gap is closed, I don't get a little pouch anymore on my lower back; however, there's no place for the fluid to go so it builds up on my brain. I had to have a way to relieve the pressure in my head; That's why I have a shunt, or a tube, in my head that everyone can see. The tube is like a little straw that takes liquid from my head to my tummy.

Who wants to give THAT explanation to a 10-year-old kid? Not me. I hate all the questions. I'm just different. But I'm just like every other kid, curious to know things too. When we go places and I see kids with a different disability, like Brittle Bone Disease, I need someone to explain why they act or look the way they do.

One time my dentist made a mistake and forgot to change his gloves and my cheeks got red and bumpy. I'm allergic to latex. I can't play with balloons either. When I was a little baby, anything with latex got taken away from me. Sometimes Mom wasn't fast enough and the little red bumps were already starting. After a little time, my skin returns to normal and I'm fine.

Last year at school I got bullied and made fun of a lot because I had to wear a diaper to school. Other kids would call me a baby and it would hurt my feelings a lot. I helped with an anti-bullying campaign Shriners Hospital put on at my school. They called the campaign: *Cut the Bull*, and I did a part of the presentation.

It's important to me that kids learn and understand that everyone has feelings. Even if some kids don't talk, or walk, or do things like a typical person can. Everybody has feelings, and we should show kindness and respect for everyone. The message I hope everyone learns from me is that I'm just like everybody else, unique in my own way. I'm just as deserving as the next kid to be included and to play. We can all be friends despite our differences.

I like to find ways to be the center of the crowd, I love people and it makes me feel good when people love me back. People often tell me that I'm very charismatic. Whenever I'm in a crowd I'm always looking to find someone to make them smile.

MY NAME IS ADRIAN.
I have SPINA BIFIDA and HYDROCEPHALUS.
What's YOUR Superpower?

Tyler

WHAT'S YOUR SUPERPOWER?

I've been told that I give others courage and that I have a great heart."

Hi, I'm Tyler. I love building things and using my hands. When I was a kid, I had K'NEX model building set, better than Lincoln Logs by far. The pieces were made of colored plastic in various shapes and sized and, when connected, I could make things like cars, skyscrapers, and pulleys. I like creating things that move. Even though I'm now an adult, I still love to eat Captain Crunch Berries cereal and eat sweet treats like Kit Kat bars.

As a child, I liked to ride my bike and race with toy cars. When I was in elementary school one of my favorite games was Four Square with the big green classroom ball. I'm 23 years old now and work as a mechanic, servicing cars at a major dealership. Now I race real cars.

When I went to college at Utah Valley University (UVU) I was in the racing club. I have an orange Dodge Neon SRT4 I like to work on and race with. Right now, I do rookie racing experiences; In the future, I'd like to be an amateur or pro racer and use a serious race car, like my favorite car the 2010 Dodge Viper. I really like watching car races, especially the International Supermodified Association (ISMA). It's similar to Grand Tour Racing or Nascar but any person can enter to race in ISMA if the car qualifies. The race isn't just for elite racers.

I can also feel vibrations and it helps me understand what's happening around me. Especially if I'm at a dance, listening to music, and when I'm at work in the auto garage.

From kindergarten to 3rd grade I rode the bus and attended a special school. One memory I have of riding the bus was the day of the super big wind storm. As I stepped off the bus the wind was blowing so hard, I felt like I was about to fly off the ground. In my first school, there were bell alarms with lights which helped everyone know when classes were over. Some of my friends couldn't hear and depended on the flashing light alarm to know when the class was finished.

I changed schools in 4th grade to attend public school. I was the only deaf student in that school. To help me learn and understand, I had an ASL interpreter all throughout school that would come with me to all of my classes. The transition into public school was a bit challenging and frustrating. Learning to communicate with hearing kids so they could understand what I was trying to say was at times pretty challenging. It got better and easier the more I would communicate with others, and for them to communicate with me, with or without using my hearing device. I had many friends in school but I didn't pay too much attention to what other kids thought of me doing sign language. I never really noticed if people were making fun of me for any reason. I mostly paid attention to my interpreter.

I have a severe sensorineural hearing loss (often called nerve deafness). When I was three years old, I had surgery on the side of my head by my ear and got a cochlear implant. I have a small piece of metal behind and above my ear, that has been placed under my skin by a doctor. I put the microphone device – doctors call it a sound processor – on top of that and, because of the little magnet, the microphone sticks on my head so I can hear. I am not actually hearing sound from my damaged ear drum but from digital information that is changed to an electrical signal and sent to my hearing nerve so my brain can understand the sound. Think of how it sounds when a computer speaks words, it sounds mechanical and not entirely "human". I can hear well, but if you were to hear the sounds I hear, you would think they are a bit distorted. To make complete sense of things, I rely a lot on looking at faces, reading lips, and gestures. When all of these puzzle pieces are put together, I hear and communicate with the world around me.

Before this, I couldn't hear anything. It was like a new part of my brain had turned on when I heard sound for the first time. Because I have one cochlear implant on the left side of my head, some people think I have unbalanced hearing, but I've never heard with both sides so this is normal to me. Some deaf people have two implants, one on each side, but getting a second cochlear can be a bit costly and I'm satisfied with the way I can hear. It has its challenges... as well as its benefits. Having a cochlear implant puts me in between two worlds, each with cultural differences. I can hear, but not completely.

In kindergarten, I learned how to speak with my hands using American Sign Language (ASL). It was hard learning how to talk and vocalize so that other people could understand me. Sounds that were hard to make with my mouth were K, F, and V. Some of my friends from the deaf and blind school can't speak, so they try to communicate with gestures or writing.

There are a few advantages to being deaf. Whenever I want to unplug from the world, I just take off my Cochlear and I'm in complete peace and silence; unless there's a vibrating jackhammer nearby. If I have a full mouth at dinner and need to talk, I use sign language and it's not impolite. However, if a hearing person talks with their mouth full it's considered impolite and rude. If I'm signing with someone, and people can't walk around me, it's okay to walk between the people signing. Some people wait or try to go around. They don't understand it's okay to quickly walk through.

Giving service to others is very fulfilling to me and brings me joy. I served as a missionary for my church in Rochester New York for two years teaching people about the Gospel of Jesus Christ. I've been told that I give others courage when they learn about me and that I have a great heart. I'm always willing to help and teach and translate for others who need ASL. It makes me feel included and valued in my community.

MY NAME IS TYLER.
I am DEAF.
What's YOUR Superpower?

Zuleika

WHAT'S YOUR SUPERPOWER?

I"ve learned not to push my pace, but to take things at my own speed."

Hi, my name is Zuleika. I live in Switzerland and can speak three different languages, English, Spanish and Italian. Listening to music and traveling are some of my favorite pastimes. I like to read and dance, even if it's a little different from other people. I like to sit and visit with my friends and cook. Some of my favorite foods are chicken salad, pizza, and doughnuts. Mmmmm!

Sixteen years ago, I had an accident that changed my life. I slipped between a dock and a moving train, landing on the tracks. The train rolled over my left arm and leg, which the doctors had to amputate to save my life.

My father would fly in from New York every 2-3 weeks in the beginning, then once every few months to be with me as I got better. I had many friends come to be with me and it helped cheer me up and lift my spirits.

I've met more people and have made lifelong friendships I never would have had, had I not been through this accident. I stayed in the hospital for a total of seven months and had a lot of physical therapy to learn how to walk again. It took three months to take a few steps, and I needed assistance. After a while, I was able to walk with a cane on my own.

Having such a traumatic experience was really hard physically and emotionally on me. I cried a lot trying to get used to my new body. I use a prosthetic arm and leg now when I go out. They hurt and I get sores on my leg because the prosthetic is so heavy. I always walk using a cane. When I'm at home or at work, I use a wheelchair to get around. The top of my leg has to be strapped around my waist and can be very uncomfortable. It throws my posture off and it hurts my back. At the end of the day, I'm exhausted from having to move my heavy artificial limb. Nobody ever told me it would be so heavy.

I've learned not to push my pace, but to take things at my own speed. I cannot run. I can type, cut vegetables, cook, cut paper, iron, wash dishes, and do my hair and make-up all with one hand, though not at the same time.

I work as an assistant at a boarding school in the alumni relations and development department. I organize reunions and help with fund-raising to benefit the school. I take trips to different places around the world. The students I work with have served in several countries. My first trip was to Romania. While we were there, the students did academic humanitarian projects to help the community, like helping to build a home and school, building shelves, painting and other projects that the village needed help with. While there, we stayed in a rustic home in the countryside. It was very pretty. It was wonderful to be of service to such a kind and grateful people. I love my job.

Whenever I travel, I always use disabled assistance. They treat me like a queen. I get picked up to ride to the airport. In Italian, it's called Sala A mica or *Friend's Room*. I love that part of traveling, interacting with my crew and building friendships. They're so warm and kind- hearted.

I am empathetic to others hardships because I have also been in

34

Zuleika

a dark place, I'm a great listener and people feel at ease around me.

MY NAME IS ZULEIKA.
I AM A DOUBLE AMPUTEE with two PROSTHETIC LIMBS.
What's YOUR Superpower?

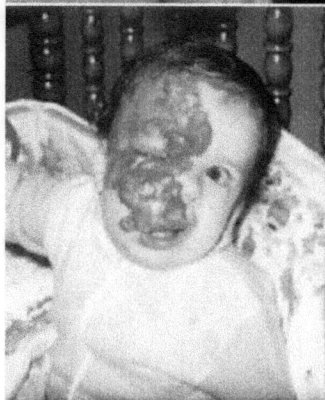 

Nate

WHAT'S YOUR SUPERPOWER?

"People often tell me I've got an eye for great pictures."

Hi, I'm Nate. I love all outdoor activities. Some of my favorites are mountain biking, hiking with my wife and kids, and camping in the Uintah's and Wind River, Wyoming. In the winter I really enjoy skiing and snowboarding at Snowbird. One unique hobby I really enjoy is spelunking. That's when people hike through, climb and explore different caves. I've even been to an underground cave created by ancient hydro-thermal activity in the earth. It was exciting, even though I nearly got stuck.

I'm musically talented and like to sing, play the French horn, trumpet and flute but the piano is my favorite. Music is one way I feel I can express myself fully. It brings me joy. I can juggle and have been known to freak people out when, without stretching, I can do perfect splits. I like being active. When I was younger, I wanted to try a Navy Seal workout that the military do to get buff; holy crap that kicked my butt!

I like lots of different foods and like to cook. Curry dishes, sushi, and Asian foods are my favorite. I cannot eat any kind of shellfish though, I'm deathly allergic.

I was born with a very small red bumpy birthmark on my cheek.

Within hours and days, it grew rapidly. Doctors did a bunch of medical tests on me to figure out what was happening. The mark went up to my hairline, my ear across my eye and down to my lip. The abnormal tissue growth looked like a *Phantom of the Opera* mask.

The doctors gave me an angiogram, a test that took a picture of my blood vesicles in my face using an x-ray. I had to get a shot that made my blood change a different color so the image would show up on the x-ray; similar to when someone dyes their hair a different color, only the dye changes the color of the blood inside my body. The dye has high levels of iodine and in some people, it causes them to have a high sensitivity to shellfish afterward; I guess that made me a "some people".

The doctors came back to tell my parents I had a hemangioma. That's a cluster or a non-cancerous tumor made up of blood vesicles on the surface of the skin. It happened before I was born and is usually harmless but typically grows for the first year. Doctors thought I had a different more severe condition called Sturge-Weber syndrome because of its growth and how it was affecting my right eye. After some months monitoring my condition, just before I turned one, doctors confirmed I did not have that.

I had glaucoma and was blind from birth in my right eye. My condition destroyed muscle tissue in my face making my eye mostly closed. I wasn't expected to live to have my 12th birthday. I was given adult doses of medications, which destroyed my immune system from all of their side effects. I was constantly sick with strep throat and had pneumonia three times before I was five. I spent a year at Primary Children's Hospital just trying to heal and function. By the time I turned six my red mark had decreased in size by 70 percent.

As I got older my eye was very sensitive to light. It hurt and I had to keep my head down. It would often sting and water a lot. Doctors said that my eye was not repairable and that I'd never be able to see through my right eye. One doctor mentioned: "Only bad would happen if I kept it" so at seven years old it was removed.

Having surgery made things a lot better. My mother said I was a whole new kid. I was very shy before. I didn't play and was not active at all. After my eye was removed, I was full of energy, rambunctious, and some would say a bit – *nuts*. My parents had a giant learning curve raising me.

We moved when I was eight and I started making friends. A few friends were very close and accepted me even though my eye was gone. I got a prosthetic eye that I could pop in and look more normal and fit in better. But it wasn't always comfortable and I'd sometimes lose it. I liked the idea of looking more normal, but it was a bit of a hassle sometimes and wouldn't always stay in.

When I was nine, my brother and I went swimming in my aunt's pool. We would play with my eye by tossing it into the pool, then dive down and try to find it. My brother was at the edge of the pool trying to spot it when a kid walked by.

He curiously asked: "What are you doing?"

"My brother's eye fell out."

The look on that kid's face was horrified and priceless. We were rolling in laughter as he ran away.

School started and so did the bullying. I had a lot of name-calling and teasing. Emotionally, I got worse and worse. My grades were dropping and I became withdrawn from people. Seventh grade was the worst social time, worse than a prison sentence. The name of my junior high school was Whalquist, but I called it Walcatraz. That was more fitting.

Nearly daily, I got into fights defending myself. They weren't physical attacks, not usually; my response was initiated by their words. So, to get them back for being mean I would punch them. My math teacher overheard me being bullied from outside the bathroom once. When I came out, he had a concerned look on his face and asked me if

I needed anything; I just said "Nope" and walked on. I never told anyone about being bullied; not my parents, not the principal, no one. It never crossed my mind that I could say something to a teacher or an adult to make it stop. I just dealt with it on my own.

Still, I was frequently in the principal's office. I felt that I had to work harder to prove I was just as smart and as good as anybody else. I had a highly overdeveloped sense for justice as a kid. If I ever saw someone else getting bullied, I'd step in to even out the score, and I'd fight for them. One of my friend's hats got stolen. I tried to make things fair and bargain with the bully to give it back but he had no desire to. So, I punched him.

As an adult, I'm still protective and caring of my friends, but I've learned how to control my actions and emotions better than when I was younger.

When I was learning how to drive, my parents and the driver's ed teacher were a bit concerned with my depth perception; but I actually am a fantastic driver. I have really good peripheral vision. Just like a wide-angle lens on a camera, I'm able to see more than what's right in front of me.

I've always been fascinated with cameras. I remember as a 4-year-old looking at my dad's SLR Camera. My mom loved the latest Olympus camera. They were always taking family pictures at parties. People often tell me I've got an eye for great pictures.

I took a trip to Costa Rica for my 22nd birthday. My friend offered to lend me his camera. It was a Pro SLR Camera. I was totally hooked! This camera was amazing and had features, unlike any camera I've ever owned. I like the science behind photography and love trying to capture fast fleeting moments. When I got back home to give the camera back, my friend shocked me by telling me that I could keep it! I was ecstatic and so grateful! It was so much fun capturing amazing images like sunsets, tropical wildlife, toucans, sloths, and poisonous dart frogs. I feel like I have a connection with things that I photograph.

Not long after, my Spanish professor saw some of my photos and asked if I would shoot his daughter's wedding. He really encouraged me to continue photography. A friend mentored me with some aspects of photography and I've been a professional photographer ever since. People often tell me I've got an eye for great pictures.

I've taken pictures of US Figure Skating, the Olympic Committee, and the Luge World Championships. I've shot on a movie set, and have taken pictures for celebrities like Danny Glover and Anthony Hopkins. I've taken photos of dignitaries like the general of the Hill Air Force Base. I met and photographed the US Airforce Thunderbirds Pilots and was even invited to the test range where they blow stuff up.

One fact about me is that I don't have perfect 20/20 vision; but I do have perfect 20 vision. I can promise you one thing for certain, I'll always keep an eye out for ya.

People tell me they are inspired when they meet me for the first time. Others often say they feel like they've known me for years, and oddly I feel the same way. I make friends fast and get to know them deeply.

MY NAME IS NATE. I have ONE EYE.
What's YOUR Superpower?

Carly

WHAT'S YOUR SUPERPOWER?

"I LOVE my birthday! It makes me feel special to have loved ones around me giving me attention and being the princess of the day."

Hi, my name is Carly. I love going to school, talking and being around friends and family. My favorite holiday is Thanksgiving. I like Christmas too, but not because of the presents. I like being around all of my family and cousins. I like reading books and going to see plays at the theatre. Joseph and the Amazing Technicolor Dream Coat is my favorite play.

I love Disney princesses and know everything about Disney shows. I love my speech therapist who helped me to talk better. My occupational therapist helped me learn to write my name and eat with a spoon. My physical therapist helped me to walk and get stronger muscles to have better balance.

I enjoy talking with Grandma on the phone. At my house, Friday night is always pizza night! Grilled cheese sandwiches are also super yummy. I love birthday parties and get excited on car ride adventures.

It makes me happy to say please and thank you. Other people are really nice to me and I enjoy being polite. I like smiling a lot and love life. When I say my prayers I always ask: "Please help us to be happy."

I LOVE my birthday! It makes me feel special to have loved ones around me giving me attention and being the princess of the day.

When I was seven days old my blood wasn't flowing correctly and the doctors had to repair a tube in my heart. When I was born parts of my skin in my lip and mouth didn't zip closed. The whole top of my mouth inside was missing and was just a big hole. I had to have a lot of surgeries growing up to fix my mouth. My face and mouth hurt a lot, but I wanted to be happy, so I was. People would always stare at me. They didn't like how I looked. Others were friendly and talked with me. I liked that.

When I was a baby, I was fed by a tube that went in my nose and down to my tummy. I didn't like it and would pull it out. At six months old a tube was put into my tummy called a GI tube, which I was fed through for most of my life. I was fed thick liquid four times a day and never tasted what I ate. I liked to suck the salt off of pretzels though. I always joked that I could eat and talk at the same time without being rude.

In 2nd grade, I got braces on my teeth and had to wear headgear until I was in junior high. I was fourteen years old when I started eating regular food.

When I was in 4th grade some of my good friends stopped coming over to visit me. It hurt my feelings. Some friendships since then haven't lasted long. I guess it's because people have different interests and move on from being my friend or they just don't know how to include me because I'm different. I just want friends, someone to come talk to me.

I grew up going to therapists and doctors and they became some of my best friends. My bones in my back were curved so I had to get surgery on my back when I was 22 to sit up straight. I like the way I look now. In old pictures I was hunched over; I'm proud to stand a little taller. I use a wheelchair and have hearing aids because I have some hearing loss.

At night I sleep with a little oxygen tube in my nose. I take acting classes with a special needs group and LOVE IT! This spring, my dream will come true. We are performing Joseph and the Amazing Technicolor Dream Coat and I'M THE NARRATOR! I've wanted to do this my whole life! Finally, at 28, I'm going to be a star!

My family always brags about how positive and happy I am. "Even when things are hard, she's extremely happy and it's hard to get her down," my mom says.

MY NAME IS CARLY.
I have a BILATERAL CLEFT LIP and PALATE, and
SCOLIOSIS.
What's YOUR Superpower?

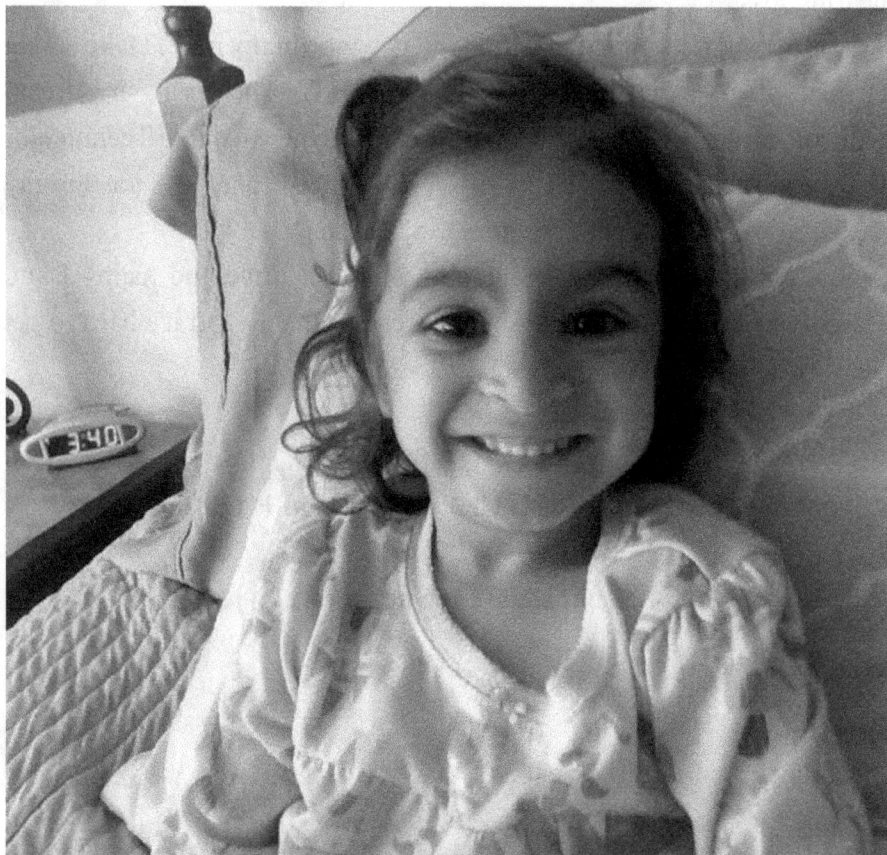

Lucy

WHAT'S YOUR SUPERPOWER?

"No matter how tiny I am, I am determined to succeed. I always work hard to accomplish my goals."

Hi, my name is Lucy. I was adopted when I was two months old from New York. I'm cute and very small. I eat a lot of pasta, ice cream, candy, pizza, chocolate, and carrots. I don't like other veggies, but carrots are my favorite. My parents are okay with me eating junk food because it's helping me to gain weight. I'm two and a half and I look like I'm only one.

I'm extremely adventurous and like to climb anything, especially trees, tables, and all furniture. I am super strong and love to play on the swings and jump on the trampoline. I love going on vacations with my family, especially if it's somewhere I can swim like a fish. Currently I'm learning my ABC's and love my bedtime stories. The *Llama Llama* kids' series and *Pig the Pug* are my favorites right now. I love my family and like spending time with my older sister who was also adopted; she's eight years old and came from China! Naomi has Down Syndrome. She's super silly and I love spending time laughing and playing with her.

My birth mother is from Russia. When I was in her tummy, she drank alcohol and used drugs. It made it really hard for my body to grow healthy. I only weighed four pounds when I was born. I was so excited to be born I came two months early! I didn't know it would be such a challenge to be alive though. I'm really lucky because some kids like me are born addicted to the yucky drugs that their mothers used when they were pregnant. I was born without withdrawals. Drugs are not good, especially for developing babies.

It's hard for me to grow and gain weight. The doctors said junk food can help my body gain weight. That hasn't happened yet, but it sure is yummy. Mommy and Daddy are lucky they get to have me as their cute little princess for a while longer, but I don't like being treated like a baby. I'm a big girl!

I'm an expert runner but got into trouble once when I ran in the street to get a quarter on the other side. I just saw something shiny, I didn't understand it wasn't safe. I get distracted and obsessed with little things that intrigue me. Mommy has this buckle that I play with. I like to open and close it a lot. It's shiny and makes a funny click noise. I'm easily entertained with things like this.

Sometimes it's hard for me to swallow. I choke on the littlest things, like a tiny crumb of broken Cheerio. Some textures feel weird in my mouth, like meat, oranges or asparagus. They are too stringy. Mommy calls them fibrous.

I learn a little slower than other kids my age. Right now, I'm learning my colors. I love ALL colors, but pink and red are my favorites today. I'm learning how to talk better, too. I have a little bit of a tongue tie which makes it difficult for me to form some sounds. That's where the bottom of the tongue has a little piece of skin that doesn't let my tongue raise up very high. I'm super smart, but I don't know as many words as other kids my same age. I have some speech and intellectual delays. Learning new things is a challenge because I'm too busy to slow down and pay attention. Mommy says I progress at my own rate, and that's okay.

I'm always on the move. I don't like sitting still. When I'm being taught something, I get SO distracted with everything and anything: a plane flying outside, a hangnail, a door closing, someone eating chips, a water bottle being crunched, a bird chirping outside, the clock ticking, my shoe is untied, the phone ringing. I'm thirsty; there's too much life to notice and tings to play with; I don't want to sit still! Sometimes I can be overwhelming to other kids. The aren't as excited about life as I am.

No matter how tiny I am, or how difficult something may be, I'm determined to succeed; like when I rode on the boogie board at the lake with my sister. Some people have said that I "Take the Bull by the horns." I always work hard to accomplish my goals. I'm happy and excited about life. I'm and expert problem solver and will work on anything challenging until I figure it out.

MY NAME IS LUCY.
I have FETAL ALCOHOL SYNDROME.
What's YOUR Superpower?

MAKE EVERY
MEAL A COMBO
ADD A RIB
SIDEKICK

Charlie

WHAT'S YOUR SUPERPOWER?

"People tell me all the time that I'm very thoughtful and generous and that I have an incredible memory."

Hi, I'm Charlie. If something interests me, I lock onto the idea and become obsessed, learning every detail about it. I really like dinosaurs and I'm an expert on them. I can tell you all their names, and special features. T-Rex, is my favorite because he's the king of the dinosaurs. He's a ferocious predator and the largest carnivore!

People tell me I'm really smart. When I was little, I loved trains! *Thomas the Train* was my favorite because the characters all have faces and different names. I don't like model trains though, they don't have faces.

I really like animals now. There's a lady where I live that is a cat lover. She brings kitties and lets me and my friends pet the kitties. I LOVE kitties, rabbits, and dogs.

When I was 23, I worked at a stable, a rescue ranch for special needs animals taking in animals who are hurt. They had sheep, horses, dogs, goats, and cats, all who had a disability. Some had a lost limb or they were blind or lame; (That means the animal can't walk or stand very well). After I did my job of feeding and brushing the horses, I put a saddle on one and got to ride it!

I love to eat shrimp with cocktail sauce, shrimp scampi, shrimp alfredo, fried shrimp, anything shrimp! Whenever my family goes out to eat, I always get a big plate full. I also like food with big flavors like lemons, hot sauce with chips, and sushi with wasabi. Wowee!

I really like to go to Planet Fitness and work out. I walk on the treadmill and watch one of my favorite shows, Law*yer* and Order – that's what I call it.

It's fun to be around other people. I'm unique because I like being social. Other friends like me mostly stick to themselves. At my last birthday, I turned 26! We went to the aquarium. My favorite exhibit was visiting the penguins. I like to watch them slide on their bellies, spin in the water, and zoom to jump out of the water. It's exciting.

I get bored fast and can't pay attention very long. Sometimes I get irritated with people if I have to wait in line and be patient. It makes me feel like I can't decide or solve a problem like I want to. I used to act in appropriate ways when I was little, kicking and screaming. Now that I'm older, if I act out, I know I can lose privileges or responsibilities that I enjoy. I try to be patient, but I still don't like waiting.

Some of my friends have seizures or heart problems. One of my best friends has kidney problems. Not me, I don't have any of those problems.

When I was 14, I moved. Now I live in a group home with a lot of friends and caregivers. I'm very close with my family, but here I can practice my independence and enjoy being around others with special needs like me.

I have a job. I used to sweep floors, but I got a promotion. There was another job that I wanted that paid more, cleaning linens. We ride a big van and collect from different schools, gyms, and kitchens. Different places that have linens like towels, washcloths, aprons, and napkins. I couldn't do that job right away because I used to drool a lot. I didn't mean to get the clean laundry dirty. I got a different medicine that helped me stop drooling so I could work. I take a different medicine to help my body stay healthy, but it makes my hands shake. We take the laundry back where we live to wash, fold and package them back up for return.

Whenever we go on a family car ride, I always give my mom directions where to go. She can't remember how to get to *Target*, but I can. I'm an expert navigator! I have sensory overload with certain things. When I was little, I didn't like wearing clothes because of how they felt on my legs and tummy. I'm hypersensitive, like with touches. I will cuddle with my mom for a few seconds, but I don't like people touching me. If someone tells me to give a hug goodbye or a high 5, I will, but I'll never ask for them myself. Some people get their feelings hurt because I'm not touchy. They think I don't like them. That's not true, I just don't give physical affection on my own.

I really like hats! People give me hats all the time. Baseball hats are my favorite. I have a fedora, and a tall one like "The Cat in the Hat". When I was little, I had a train conductor hat.

My community is great and I don't get made fun of or bullied. I'm accepted for who I am. My disabilities are celebrated, I'm just like everyone else. I speak very well, but I don't say complete sentences, I leave out words. "You Understand?"

One thing that's unique about me is that I am aware of other people's feelings. If one of my buddies is crying, I'll ask, "You hurt?" but I won't go give him a hug. Sometimes I hear people talk and want to sound cool like them. Sometimes I get in trouble and say inappropriate things like swear words or different movie lines like from *Transformers* or *South Park*. When I start a quote, I have to finish the whole thing, Mom can't stop me in the middle. It makes people laugh and I feel accepted, so I do it more! Sometimes Grandma doesn't like the words I use, and I tell her sorry. I notice when there's a pregnant mommy around. I'll ask, "When you hatch?"

I like to make different craft projects. I made a little blanket for my new baby cousin. I tied knots in the fringe of the fabric. It had duck pictures. I like making different things and giving them away as presents. I do that because I know it's nice to give people things, so I do it too. I love making bead bracelets and necklaces and rings. I always have necklaces and chains on. I like jewelry from the dollar store. I make things for myself and for my family, but not other people too much. There is one girl that I'll give things to. She's in a wheelchair. She's African American and is a good friend.

I memorize movies, repeating them like a parrot. Some of my favorites are Jurassic Park and live action movies. I love Pokémon! I have a book with thousands of cards, and I've memorized all the names. I may not say my sentences completely but I can perfectly pronounce the dinosaur named Parfilofisauris. People tell me all the time that I'm very thoughtful and generous and that I have an incredible memory.

MY NAME IS CHARLIE.
I have AUTISM.
What's YOUR Superpower?

Emmalynn

WHAT'S YOUR SUPERPOWER?

"...my laughter is contagious. When I was a baby, I used to wake up in the middle of the night laughing. I've realized it's comforting to me. Laughing is one thing I can do that I have control over. It gives me peace."

Hi, I'm Emmalynn. I love being outside in the fresh air and feeling the wind on my face. Swinging, laying on the trampoline to get bounced, and sitting outside are some of my favorite activities. Just being outside makes me happy. When I hear some of my favorite songs come on the radio, like Katy Perry or Maroon 5, I get super excited and have to dance. I dance more with my arms than my legs, swinging them all around. Even though they are a little stiff I still have fun.

Some of my favorite foods now are pizza, flavored popcorn, and tacos! I'm a taco lovin' kid and love meat! When we go on trips my mom always brings my favorite snack, Goldfish crackers. These haven't always been my favorite foods though. I use to not even know what a *favorite food* was.

My family plays with me a lot and make me feel loved. They like to make me smile, and think it's funny when I laugh, so they tickle me more. I like it when people touch and tickle me, it makes me feel like they love me. Sometimes I'll go over to my dad and move his hand so he will tickle me more.

Sometimes I don't feel very good and just like to snuggle with my mom or dad, or lay down with my younger sister. I use a wheelchair to get around, and I don't talk. I'm trying to practice my sounds more though.

Immediately after I was born my mom knew that something wasn't right. I was very floppy like a rag doll and didn't have much muscle tone like other babies. Then I would pull my arms and legs into my body and tense up and stay like that. I didn't feel good, I didn't know what my body was doing. It would make me hurt but I didn't know why, so all I could do was cry… a lot. Mommy tried and tried to make me feel better, but nothing helped. I wish I could have told her what I was feeling.

At four weeks old the doctors told my mom I had Failure to Thrive syndrome. Most babies get chubby really fast; I should have been gaining weight, but I was losing weight, so I had to be put on a special type of formula until I was a year old, then I started to eat regular food.

The first hospital, where we spent the most time, seemed to disregard that something wasn't right. I was still too little for them to believe there were any problems with me. "Each child develops at their own rate, she'll eventually catch up," one doctor said. They thought I seemed healthy and couldn't find anything wrong. Daily I got worse.

I would have staring spells and zone out; It was like a message was trying to be sent across my brain but there was a roadblock and the message never got sent. So, my brain would try again and again, misfiring time after time. Sometimes I would jerk my arms and legs, but the movements were small. Barely noticeable. My Mom noticed.

When I saw people, I didn't look at their faces because I almost felt like I wasn't connecting with my body like I should. I was fuzzy in my head and couldn't make sense of things. People would talk to me, but it's like they were talking from really far away even though they were right next to me. I couldn't acknowledge they were even there. I would stare at something, but I didn't know what it was that I was looking at.

I would often stare at the ceiling light, laughing. I didn't know what this ball of light was but I couldn't stop laughing it made me so happy. It made me think and feel that maybe somehow it could help me communicate; and I felt that there were others (my family) close to me, and through the laughter, I could feel them.

I was like a premature baby, small and not developing or progressing. I stayed that way until I was six months old. That's when they realized there was a problem. They did several tests on me, thinking the issue may be seizures: a sudden uncontrolled electrical disturbance in the brain.

Every test came back normal. They knew something was off, but they didn't know what. Some of my symptoms acted like a seizure symptom, but they could not capture it on any of the tests. I was put on a seizure medication to see if it would help me. Mom was very frustrated with no answers.

Not long afterward I was acting strangely again; it was worse than before. My head would drop down and I'd become completely unresponsive. I'd reopen my eyes, confused and dazed 30-40 seconds later. It's like I was repeatedly passing out. This happened off and on for 10 minutes. It's like my brain computer was trying to reboot and it kept failing. It freaked my mom out and she called 911 and asked which hospital to take me to, NOT wanting to go back to the other hospital. They told her to go to Children's Memorial Herman Hospital in Houston, Texas.

"That was the best decision I ever made," Mom tells people. "Finally, there were physicians that we felt were listening and actually helped my daughter feel better."

At the second hospital, they re-ran all of the tests from the previous hospital, but something changed; I was currently having an episode and they were able to catch it during one of the tests! Finally, I had a diagnosis...an answer. Part of my struggle? I was autistic.

In 2014 the new doctors discovered and officially diagnosed me with epilepsy as well. I was put on high strength adult doses of epilepsy medications in an attempt to control the seizures in my brain. As with all medications, it came with side effects.

I was having up to 300 seizures a day. They were unnoticeable, they happened in clusters or twitches, and it was all in my brain. My body and brain had so much stress from the seizures and chemical overload I had no desire for food, I just wanted to feel better. When I was three years old, I stopped eating. In 2015 I got a Gastrostomy (G-tube) put in my tummy so I could eat and stay alive. I ate this way for the next two years.

It wasn't until November 2016 that I was diagnosed with EIEE, a rare genetic disorder: Early Infantile Epileptic Encephalopathy. Try saying THAT three times fast.

I was four years old when I first started to engage with people; the first time I made eye contact with my mom. I tried to communicate with small gestures. Sometimes I would interact with others; most of the time I just sat looking around and trying to make sense of the sights and sounds around me. It was odd for my body to feel so distant and disconnected but on rare occasions, I could feel how close they really were. It's like my spirit was seeing for my body.

My mom and dad were continually searching for ways to help me. In June of 2017, they seriously started looking into CBD* oil. Studies and tests have shown that the oil creates positive results for others with seizures like me. They were very cautious because it was still an unknown, new therapy, but they were willing to try anything if it would help me. They learned there are different plants that have this beneficial natural medicine inside them…

So, when I started another visible seizure; With a lot of hope, they gave me 10 drops of this natural medicine in my G-tube; and it's like I was waking up for the first time. Immediately, within seconds, the seizure stopped. I started laughing and was a happy kid again. The medicine controlled my seizures and helped my brain to work more normally. I also did not have any pain.

Daily I was showing more and more improvement. Shortly after I started using CBD drops, I started making eye contact with people. I'm actually trying to talk when before I was silent. I WANT to speak. I'm eating better and have a good appetite, heck, I want to eat all day long now! I still have my G-tube, but only use it to take medicine or when my body needs water and I don't want to drink. CBD allows my brain to function more normally.

I can handle public places and crowds now, when before I would have high anxiety and it would trigger meltdowns and put my body into another seizure. Now I can be in public environments. I'm calm and actually enjoy paying attention to my surroundings. I'm acting more and more like a little kid, even though I have the attention span of a crazy little puppy running all over the place.

I stood for the first time by myself when I was six years old. I'm seven now and learning to walk better. I'm still pretty unstable and need full support but I'm taking steps! I'm walking! I'm so excited that I'm finally able to function and use my body better.

I feel better all-around because of the CBD drops I use, and, as time goes by, my health problems seem to be fading away. I'm off of a majority of the prescription medications the doctors prescribed and free from all their side effects too. I felt a huge difference when one by one, I stopped needing to take them anymore. My mom often tells people, "I feel very lucky to call Emmalynn my child. I truly believe if she'd had one more sickness she would have died. I give CBD credit for saving her life."

I am a super big cuddle bug. I love to snuggle and get loves from my family and just be together. My mom is my rock. I like to laugh, and randomly bust out laughing because I catch the giggles; that happens a lot. Everyone else in my house starts laughing too; I guess my laughter is contagious. When I was a baby, I used to wake up in the middle of the night laughing. I've realized it's comforting to me, laughing is one thing I can do that I have control over and gives me peace.

MY NAME IS EMMALYNN.
I have AUTISM and EPILEPSY.
What's YOUR Superpower?

*Marijuana (cannabis) and hemp (cannabidiol or CBD) – of the two, hemp is less strong and the easiest to extract the THC out of. That's the hallucinogen part or the part of the plant that makes you 'high'. CBD is legal to use, unlike cannabis is in several states. Emmalynn was continually monitored by doctors and has been tested several times to determine if her body has any signs of THC. Every test has come back negative.

Ben & Sophie

Sophie & Ben

WHAT'S YOUR SUPERPOWER?

"Because of our parents, we have the ability and freedom to do anything our heart's desire, go wherever we wish and have our independence."

Hi, I'm Sophie, and this is my brother, Ben. We both grew up in an orphanage in Ukraine. When I was three years old my parents came to my orphanage and fell in love with how adorable I was. They also planned on adopting Ben who was five years old and in the same group as me; the longer they stayed, however, the greater came the feeling we weren't the only ones they were supposed to bring home.

When they went to get Ben, he had been moved to an older group, and that's where they found our four other siblings. Mom and Dad had to come back a year later to adopt them though; The adoption paperwork only allowed for two children to be adopted. (Our parents are kicking themselves for not changing that from the beginning).

Nine of us are now adopted; I'm the baby of my family. We all have different birth mothers but our forever family is our heaven on earth.

I have a unique talent and love to paint, but I do it with my mouth, not my hands. I hold the paintbrush with my teeth and lips to dip in the paint and move my head back and forth across the canvas. I like painting faces. Those are my favorite. It's fun to create stories too! I have a computer program that allows me to talk into a microphone and it writes out the words on the computer.

I really like music and singing. I'm always singing. I was recently accepted into the elite choir in my junior high school with Ben! "The Little Drummer Boy" is my favorite song. We're rehearsing for our next concert. We really like going to orchestra and choir concerts with our family. Music calms me and makes me feel free.

Swimming is another fun pastime. I love to feel weightless in the water when I move my arms and legs. We have a pool, but it's hard to get into. When my family goes on vacation we always stay at a hotel with a pool. Mom and Dad are always my swimming buddies.

My favorite thing to eat is salads! Not just any old salad, my mom's gourmet chef's salad. It has Spinach, chicken, blueberries, strawberries, and feta cheese with strawberry vinaigrette. Mmmmm. Strawberry salad is another favorite.

Ben loves cars! He likes matchbox cars, seeing pictures of cars, looking at cars, EVERYTHING about cars. He has a dream to one day work at a fancy auto dealership and shine all of the amazing cars there.

We live on top of a hill at the edge of a forest. We have a lot of land where Dad does a type of gardening called Aquaponics. Ben likes to help out with carrying the toolbox, holding the lamp for Dad and handing him screws to build new growing beds. He likes to feel helpful and handy.

Whenever we have enchilada or taco night for dinner Ben LOVES it. He likes spicy foods. Another favorite is Indian food, with curry, red pepper or chili powder. He doesn't go seeking out hot things, like putting extra Tabasco on tacos. However, if Mom over spices dinner with chili powder he really enjoys it. He also has a bit of a sweet tooth, always sneaking cookies.

Sophie & Ben

When my brother and I were born we had a rare disease that caused some of our joints to be curved or *hooked*. It's called arthrogryposis (AMC). We had multiple contractures, or shortened muscles making our joints stick and bend inward. For me, my feet, legs, hands, and arms were affected. When I came home to the USA at three years old, I could not roll over, sit up, walk, or dress. I could scoot and stay sitting but only if someone sat me up. My legs and feet were bent inward. If you put your hands on your hips like Superman and look down at your arms, pretend those are your legs. That's what mine looked like.

In my life, I've had over 10 different surgeries to correct my body structure so I can move easier and be able to walk. Doctors cut and turned the top bone in my leg so my feet would face forward. They also fixed my tendon in the bottom of my leg so my clubbed feet could relax down and not bend inward. My hands and arms also had surgery to re-position the bones to look and function more naturally. One surgery took three months per leg to heal; it helped my bone get longer and corrected the shape. It's named after the doctor who invented it, the Illizarov Fixator. My leg was put into an 8-ring stabilizer attached to my leg bone.

My Parents thought my condition would be an *easy fix* and they would have a normal child. Even though I'm highly intelligent with no cognitive delays, AMC is a lifelong condition. I also have a condition called amylophagia which means that some muscles didn't form at all before I was born. I have no bicep muscles in the top of my arm and no quadricep muscles in the top of my legs. I can't bend or flex my arms up to brush my teeth or eat food. To walk I use Knee Ankle Foot Orthotics (KAFO) braces from my foot all the way up to the very top of my legs. My braces hold me up.

I'm now 13 years old and stand 4'5" tall. My height (as well as Ben's) was stunted because of our genetic condition and living in an orphanage. I learned how to walk when I was six years old after all of my leg surgeries. When I travel outside of my home, like to school, stores or family events, I use a motorized wheelchair. My favorite part of my chair is the ability to go fast. It's exciting and fun. It's easy to move my joystick on my wheelchair, but other things are a bit more challenging, such as when I use my hands and fingers.

People are always amazed at the things I CAN do, like pick up small things, or play with little toys, write, draw, and put puzzles together. My fingers all contract down toward my arm and I move my fingers side to side to pinch and pick things up. I have no use of *Thumby;* he just hangs out in my palm. I use both of my hands all the time, usually, one hand helps the other, like when I carry my notebook or paint pad. I cross my arms and hold it against my body.

When I eat, I'll sometimes use a special fork that I scoop my food up in, then I rest my arm on the table and bring my head down to eat with my mouth. I can't raise my arms. Sometimes it's easier to just put my head down to my plate to eat right off of it. I like eating neatly and keeping my face pretty and clean, which surprises people when they see how I eat.

Ben's AMC is less severe than mine. His legs, feet, and hands are affected; his hips are a little wonky too. My brother is 15 years old and is 5'1" tall. He's only had three surgeries. Each foot had a tendon release surgery called a tenotomy to help correct his club feet so they weren't stuck sideways. He wears Ankle Foot Orthotics (AFO) braces too. His are shorter and only go from his foot to just below his knee. He has almost no muscle in his lower leg and the braces help him with stability to walk with his club foot. Ben uses a manual wheelchair part of the time for school and other outings, just like me.

He was also born with fetal alcohol syndrome (FAS) because his birth mother drank alcoholic drinks while she was pregnant with him.

Ben does everything slowly. He walks slow, processes slow, talks slow; he completes tasks slowly, he eats slow; but on his bike, he can GO FAST! It makes him feel free. Racing down the hill at our house is one of his most favorite things to do.

Ben has an awesome 3-wheel bike that he takes up to the top of our hill. Once there, he turns around and flies down with no brakes. I think he's little crazy; that would scare me to death. He sure has fun, though he does NOT like amusement parks. Every once in a while, when Ben feels strong and adventurous, he'll take his bike out to the forest by our home.

Ben was in a talent contest at school. Everyone was surprised when they saw him playing the piano. Nobody knew he could do that. He only knows a few songs but his song, *Heart*, by the band, *Alone*, blew everyone away.

He loves animals and used to have a bunny he raised from birth that he named Champagne, but he died. We have an epic secret at our house right now; he's getting a new bunny for his birthday!

When we go to the park other kids have asked him why he wears braces on his legs; "Because I got bitten by a shark" he's teased. He says the silliest things all the time. like yesterday he mentioned that he was losing his sweet tooth for chocolate. "Raspberries are hairy. I like hairy berries."

He says endearing things so often. He's sweet, gentle, kind and caring. As much as he loves treats, he makes sure Mom never goes without getting a treat too. If we have one cookie left, he will hide it to give to Mom.

Whenever I go to the park it seems as though people are attracted to me and come visit. It's common and nice when they tell me I have a pretty smile and they're happy to see me. I have a special bond with my mom, we can read each other at a glance. It's like I can tell her things without saying a word, and she completely understands.

Because of our parents, we have the ability and freedom to do anything our heart's desire, go wherever we wish and have our independence. We are so thankful to them for adopting us and all our siblings and giving us a life, we never would have had. Mom and Dad, thank you from all of our hearts.

WE ARE SOPHIE & BEN.
We have ARTHROGRYPOSIS.
What's YOUR Superpower?

Mickelle

WHAT'S YOUR SUPERPOWER?

"I like to drive my wheelchair into all of the driveways and do doughnuts. I twirl and have fun being a big girl, wearing lots of pink things and of course my favorite red sparkle Dorothy shoes. I played Dorothy from the Wizard of Oz in a school play a few years ago. I like being in costume and still wear it for fun."

Hi, I'm Mickelle. My I-Pad is my favorite toy! With one finger I feel like I can control the world in the palm of my hand. I love going to amusement parks like Lagoon in Utah. I like roller coasters, but I got scared last time when I did the upside-down ride. I thought I was going to die!

I'm obsessed with Disneyland! It brings me great joy to see and hug the characters from my favorite movies. I have a pillowcase with Ana on one side and Elsa on the other. I make my mom flip the pillow to the Ana side because I think Elsa has a scary face. It makes me giggle when my mom flips the pillow.

I'm adventurous and LOVE swimming. I feel completely weightless and can move freely without any restrictions. I just turned 20 years old and I keep wishing I could go traveling on an airplane somewhere. I always have my suitcase packed and make sure it's with me wherever I go. I never know when I'll have a surprise trip and have to leave right away! It has to be with me in the living room, my bedroom, when we sit together to eat, or take any car rides. My trusty silver case is never out of sight. Maybe next year when I blow out the candles, I'll get my wish!

I'm creative and like doing art and craft projects every day. Drawing with bright colors and every kind of paint you can imagine is one of my passions. It makes me happy. I'm very visual and don't like it when I see people with mean faces. It's almost like I can see their soul and know how they are feeling; it makes me feel sad and scared.

When I was a tiny baby in my mommy's tummy, she got sick with cytomegalovirus *(*CMV*)* when she was four months pregnant with me. It's a common virus, anyone can get it. Once someone has it, they have the virus for life. My body wasn't very healthy when my mom got sick, and it affected how I developed as a baby. The day Mommy caught that virus was the same day my brain was affected and became damaged.

I had to eat through a tiny tube that went under my belly button. I was breastfed, then shortly after that I got a gastric feeding tube (G-tube) sometimes called a *Button*. I was put on continual feed as a baby, being fed 22 out of 24 hours a day. Now that I'm older I get a feeding syringe with my food right into my G-tube every few hours.

I've had over 33 different procedures and surgeries to help my body function like it should. One surgery I'm about to get will help me so I won't drool anymore, and that will be nice. I can open and close my mouth, but I can't swallow my own spit. In the surgery, the doctor will remove the glands in my chin. I need this operation because I get wet and cold on the front of my shirt. Even though I wear large bibs across my front, they need to be changed several times a day to keep them from being soaked. I get sick often in the winter because the top of my shirt and chest stays wet and cold.

Mickelle

I've almost died over 100 times. One time I choked on a Cheerio because I couldn't swallow. If I'd died, it would have been kind of funny when I got to heaven. When they asked me how I died I'd have to tell them… "Death by Cheerio."

The scariest time for my mom was when I was 11 months old. One day when I was being placed into my crib, my G-tube cord got stuck on the end of the bed and it ripped out. When this happens, others have 20 minutes to get it placed in again or it will need to be medically done and could cause problems. My mom tried to get the tube back in but I had collapsed. I had thrown up and because my tummy was being pushed, I was throwing up again. They continually had to keep my head elevated so no fluid would go down my throat.

I nearly choked and was close to aspirating. (That's when spit-up is breathed into the lungs which is dangerous). Then I stopped breathing. One of our neighbors was a nurse and came to help Mom. The nurse stayed, keeping me alive until the ambulance came. I had an emergency surgery to get my G-tube placed again.

When I was 10 years old, I had surgery to fix my back. I had scoliosis. Most people's backbones are straight up and down, but some people like me have a sideways curved back. The doctors put two rods in my back from the top of my neck all the way down to the bottom with 18 screws to keep my spine straight. That was another emergency surgery. I was sitting so crooked that it crunched off my G-tube making it impossible for me to eat. My body wasn't absorbing any food. My food would be syringed into my G-tube and I'd throw it all up. Since I can't swallow food, I rely on being fed this way to live. I may have died had I not had that surgery. Now I sit taller. Recovery took a while, but I feel a lot better and eat a lot better now that I'm not hunched over.

I'm tall and skinny, but I don't stand. I'm 5'8" tall and weigh 105 lbs. When I need to move to the couch or into my motorized wheelchair someone in my family or one of my nannies picks me up like a baby to

75

sit me somewhere else. I make the sign for suitcase so they remember to always keep it next to me so that I'm ready for my anticipated surprise trip.

I have so much fun using my motorized wheelchair! It's great to feel independent and move fast. One of my favorite things is when we go on walks. I like to drive my wheelchair into all of the driveways and do doughnuts. I twirl and have fun being a big girl, wearing lots of pink things and of course my favorite red sparkle Dorothy shoes. I played Dorothy from the Wizard of Oz in a school play a few years ago. I like being in costume and still wear it for fun.

I feel like I fit in with my friends. The girls in my neighborhood talk to me and include me in everything. My absolute best friend is my sister Maddie. We'll cuddle in bed and hold hands. It makes me happy when I can do something to make my friends laugh. I love people and I don't realize I'm different than them. I want the same things that are important to my friends and family, like when we go out to a restaurant to eat a fun treat. They all got their pancakes and I look down in front of me waiting for mine; to realize I don't eat like them. It makes me feel sad and disappointed, even though they were including me. Sometimes my spirit longs for more than what my body is able to experience.

They say that I laugh like Chewbacca from Star Wars. Even though I can't hear – I was also born with profound hearing loss – I am audible and make sounds with my mouth. I've watched *Signing Time* so much I know some sign language, but I can't form the signs, as well as other people can; so, I just make up my own sign language. My family plays a lot of charades with me attempting to understand what I'm trying to tell them. It's fun. They make me laugh so much.

I have a unique talent; I can see angels.

I remember one Sunday in church I got so excited, I was completely joy-filled! I couldn't believe what my eyes were seeing! They were right in front of me! I told my mom in ASL what was happening because she couldn't see them. She didn't know why I was so excited. Angels were in front of me all dressed in white! They were talking to me for at least five minutes! It was amazing! When I see the angels around my house they are in normal clothes, but in church, they are all in white.

Another time when I was in the ER, I saw several angels. They were there to help the people who were being brought into the ER. They always give me great joy and comfort when I see them. I always try to get my mom to look when they come. They're all around. I never realized that not everyone can see them, which is strange to me.

Everyone I meet tells me how much I've touched their life. I don't understand why. I'm just being myself in the best way I know how, and loving life. It's nice when people can feel how much I love them.

MY NAME IS MICKELLE.
I have CEREBRAL PALSY, and I am PROFOUNDLY DEAF.
What's YOUR Superpower?

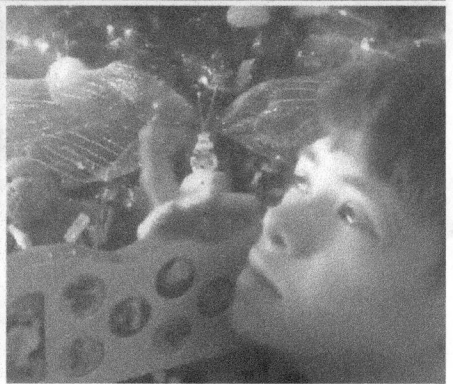

Ryker

WHAT'S YOUR SUPERPOWER?

"...life frequently filled me with laughter, love, tickles, and kisses. I'm overwhelmed with gratitude for all of the people who cared for me."

Hi, my name is Ryker. I loved going to junior high school on the bus and enjoyed taking music classes. I played the drums, the guitar and sang in the choir. When I got home from school, I liked to play with toys that make noise or played music.

One of my very favorite toys that always made me laugh was my Lilly Dog. She was a musical stuffed animal we could download songs on to. I would push her paw, then lay down with my ear to her tummy to listen to the music. When I watched TV, I turned the volume up really loud.

Christmas music was my favorite. I used to laugh when my sisters would snuggle and sing loudly, *Jingle Bells* or *Up on the Housetop*, right into my ear. I liked it loud, it made me smile and laugh.

Licking ice cream was a fun and tasty treat; but I didn't eat it, just a lick or two. I liked being home and knowing that people were around me. It was comforting. I liked being barefooted, but my feet were always cold, so everyone tried to keep socks on me. I really didn't like socks, so I ripped them off after a few minutes. I LOVED it when my dad or brothers played *This Little Piggy* with my toes.

My family used to take me with them when they went to soccer games and tournaments, but I didn't like it. I could feel the competition and tension and it would make me upset. As a baby I would get so upset I cried and turned blue, and we had to go to the hospital again. So instead of going on a family sports trip, I would stay with my nurse at home and play. I liked having a happy peaceful home where everything was familiar.

When I was born, I had a heart defect that affected how my blood flowed inside my body. Most people's skin looks pinkish from the oxygen in the air they breathe. My heart defect wasn't letting my body use the oxygen like it was supposed to, and my skin would turn pale or bluish, especially when I cried or became stressed.

I had heart surgery to help my body work better. That was the first of 34 surgeries I would have in my life. I lived at Primary Children's Hospital for a year after I was born. For four months after my heart surgery, I was hooked up to a breathing machine; I couldn't breathe on my own. The doctors tried a few times to see if I would breathe on my own, and would turn it off for a moment, but my body wasn't strong enough to breathe by myself yet.

One day at the hospital a little boy across from me was getting off of his breathing machine. He wasn't breathing. The Nurse had to do CPR and they tried to help him breathe to stay alive, but he died. After the nurse consoled that family, she came over to my mom with a serious choice that needed to be made.

After witnessing that, my mom decided the only way to keep me alive was to ask the doctors to put a tracheotomy in my throat. I was 10 months old when I had that surgery. The doctors made a little hole in my throat and put in a special tube. I was having a hard time breathing, my nose was swollen and plugged up and I couldn't clear my throat when I coughed, so this was the only way I could breathe and live. I also wore an oxygen tube in my nose.

As I got older and more mobile, I had a really long oxygen tube that allowed me to go wherever I wanted around my house and still breathe well. Every once in a while, when I had a frog in my throat and couldn't cough it out, Mom would suction my trach. It was kind of like the little vacuum they use in your mouth at the dentist office, then I could breathe better again.

I had to have 24-hour care either from my family or an at home nurse because sometimes I would pull out my trach. It would bug me and I didn't understand that I had to leave it in to help me stay alive. My oxygen levels had to be monitored all the time.

I couldn't eat food in my mouth. After I was born, I had to be fed with a tube that went from my nose to my tummy. I didn't like it. As a baby, I was always pulling it out. When I was one-year old I had another surgery to get a gastrointestinal (GI) tube put into my tummy just above my belly button on my left side. This is how I got my food. My parents, one of my siblings, or my nurse would feed me every two hours through a syringe into my GI tube. It looked like a vanilla milkshake.

When I was older, and whenever I had to have medicine, my family would tell me it was cotton candy or strawberry milk to make it funner for me. I never tasted it though; it went right into my tummy.

When I was really little, if I ever got sick and got a fever, my mom would have to watch me really closely. As soon as my temperature hit 100 degrees, I would have seizures; I would shake like I was freezing. After 45 minutes, I would pass out. This happened once every season, but Mom learned how to take care of me best. Mom would wrap me in a tight blanket to help my body calm down. She'd sing to me, and hold me until I woke up.

I didn't talk and had limited hearing. I would say jibber jabber words like Ma-ma or Daba-daba. Those were my favorite words. I didn't use sign language but was always able to communicate what I

81

wanted to my family and caregivers. I could always tell if someone was sad, mad or upset, and I didn't like that feeling, it scared me or made me upset. My family always made our home a calm, happy place for me to live.

I learned to walk when I was eight years old; that surprised the doctors too.

My brothers and I had a lot of fun at home wrestling and tickling. We freaked the nurses out all the time when they saw us wrestling. They thought I was fragile, but I was a normal fun- loving, rambunctious little boy. I liked to spin around in the twirly chair and feel the motion. I also liked toys that vibrated or buzzed. I'd put my head on them because I could feel and learn more from the vestibular stimulation. I always enjoyed it when friends or family would sing or play the guitar or piano for me. I'd sit under the piano, leaning on it to feel the vibrations. Music was a big part of my life.

One way I'd express myself or show people I loved them was a little silly. I'd pull their hair. Sometimes I'll bite, pinch or headbutt people. It's not positive or negative. I didn't do it to be mean or hurt them, it was just the way I expressed that I was happy, sad, excited, frustrated, and other feelings. I loved to give kisses and laugh and always loved to hear people sing to me. It brought me great joy.

The doctors were surprised when I lived for one year. They didn't expect me to have a party for my 3rd birthday, 5th birthday, and 12th birthday. My 13th birthday was my last birthday on earth, just before I turned 14. I went home to heaven and had an awesome birthday party there.

I lived an amazing, exciting, adventurous life. There was never a dull moment, and life frequently filled me with laughter, love, tickles, and kisses. I'm overwhelmed with gratitude for all of the people who cared for me. If you were to ask my family about me, this is what they would say:

Ryker

"Ryker was extremely loving. He had a fast bond with many people, even our foreign exchange students. You could always feel his love and he never said a word. It was more than words with Ryker. We wouldn't trade our life with him for anything."

MY NAME IS RYKER.
I had DOWN SYNDROME.
What's YOUR Superpower?

Jeff

WHAT'S YOUR SUPERPOWER?

*"I had a passion for music and loved the power of creation it gave me…
when I played my violin, it's like my worries… all went away and I could
just feel the music. When I moved to a different school as a freshman, I
went to audition for the orchestra. With my longboard in one hand and
my violin in the other, I turned quite a few heads, especially from the
conductor."*

Hi, I'm Jeff. I was born in Okinawa, Japan, in 1993 to a military family.
We lived there overseas until I was two years old. My dad was in the
air-force flying KC135 airplanes.

I grew up experiencing new things wherever we moved to and
loved the different foods of the world. Lobster and artichokes were a
couple of my very favorite things to eat; but no tomatoes. I liked trying
new things and was fearless. One of the strangest things I've ever eaten
was octopus. Asian food is awesome and I've had all sorts of different
things like Yakisoba – a popular Japanese noodle dish with meat and
vegetables.

Our favorite place to eat was a small shop with two little old
ladies. We had to pay for our food by using a vending machine. I also
really like hot foods, like salsa. Man, could I raid the refrigerator.

I became an expert skateboarder and started riding when I was five years old. I got a really nice high-quality board for Christmas one year that became one of my best friends. I named my board, Theresa. I rode every day with my friends and constantly learn new tricks. It was exciting.

When my family moved to Virginia Beach, Virginia, I learned how to surf. I was really good at it because it was just like skateboarding, only in water! My grandmother even came out to surf with me. She surfed till she was in her 60s. Some of my favorite places to surf were Lagoona Beach, California where my aunt lives, and in Texas at the Gulf of Mexico. My family and I have always been super close and we enjoy experiencing new things wherever we move.

I loved doing different activities and learned how to play the violin when I was in 4th grade. I got really good and was in the orchestra all throughout junior high and high school. I had a passion for music and loved the power of creation it gave me. I had dyslexia though and had to work at reading and speaking things correctly, but when I played my violin, it's like my worries of dyslexia all went away and I could just feel the music. When I moved to a different school as a freshman, I went to audition for the orchestra. With my longboard in one hand and my violin in the other, I turned quite a few heads, especially from the conductor.

When I played video games with my friends and family I would frequently win when we were playing as double players. That was one of my favorite evening activities when it was time to be inside for the night. I'd have video game wars with my brother and totally kick his butt. Hahaha.

On June 22, when I was 15 years old, I went to scout camp and I had an absolute blast! I was working to get my Eagle Scout award. Our first day we did rock climbing. I passed my swim test and went on a bike ride.

I had a bike accident that broke the top part of my arm by my bicep muscle. When we went to the hospital and they did x-rays, the doctors came back with some shocking news. The reason my arm had been so big and sore before my accident was because there'd been a tumor on my bone called an osteosarcoma. It's the most common form of bone cancer. Normally the cells in the tumor would have made new bone tissue, but instead, it made my bone weaker. When I fell my arm broke right through the middle of the tumor. It really hurt, but because I had never broken a bone before, I didn't know this wasn't like any other bone break.

After some tests, the doctors told us that it was cancerous. They had a plan to repair my arm. After having 12 weeks of chemotherapy to kill the cancer off, I would have bone transplant surgery. At the time we lived in Iowa. I was seen at the University of Iowa Hospital. Dr. Joe Buckwalter is one of the world's top bone cancer specialists and pioneered bone replacement surgery. I felt hopeful that everything would turn out well, and I'd be back on my skateboard in no time. I had to have a drainage pump hooked up to my arm, and wheeled it around if I needed to move. I named it *R2D2*.

Hospital food was awful! ... So, I ordered Jimmy Johns delivery and Texas Roadhouse a lot. People constantly asked where I got the steak and ribs. I brought *Theresa the Skateboard* and kept it in the window of my hospital room. That was my motivation to get better so I could go back and be a normal kid again. When I had to deal with stress, I'd go to the parking garage and roll down the parking lot, speeding down the ramps all the way to the bottom. Then I'd take the elevator back up to do it again.

I was the oldest and biggest patient in the children's ward at the hospital. While I was there, I wanted to make the best use of my time, so I went around to visit all of the other children. I would hang out in the big playroom, read them stories, and play race car. It made me feel like being a kid. That's all I wanted to be. I felt happy that I could serve them and bring a smile to their faces. They looked up to me like I was their big brother and asked me to play all the time.

Looking back before I knew I had cancer, things started making sense. I was sluggish and looked a little gray and sickly. I wanted to play and ride my skateboard over just sitting home like a lump on a log. So, I stayed active and happy, even though I felt like crap sometimes. Every afternoon I would crash at home and would take two-hour long naps. All my friends didn't understand why I was sleeping in the middle of the day.

After they treated the cancer the doctors told me that a bone transplant would not work because the chemo had failed. The cancer in my tumor was still active. I had some choices to make. The bone graft would let me keep my arm, but I wouldn't have any use of it. The only way to cure the cancer was to remove it. I thought to myself, "It's better to live without an arm than to suffer from the pain and have a dead fish arm I can't use," so I had my arm amputated.

The night before I became *disarmed,* I stayed up all night playing Halo with my friends and brothers until 5 a.m. It was AWESOME! We made great memories and talked about life and how things would be after my disarming. One of my friends had an idea to re-construct an Xbox controller to accommodate a one-handed player. His dad was an engineer and constructed it for me. I was still able to beat everyone's butt at the games. My parents still have the re-engineered controller it at home; it's pretty awesome.

Bethany Hamilton, the one-armed surfer, heard about me and sent me a package shortly before I went into surgery. She 'd been bitten by a shark and had lost her arm. I received a book and CD about how to surf with one arm. The letter of encouragement she wrote me was life-transforming and gave me incredible strength and hope. It's because of her that I knew I was going to be okay and would get back to living life to the fullest.

At the end of September of that year, the doctors amputated everything all the way up to the ball and socket of my shoulder. They wanted to make sure all of the cancerous parts of bone were completely gone. Seven days after my amputation I was home. I still had staples and stitches in my arm. I kept telling my dad, "I just want to be a kid! Let me be a kid!" and just like that, I was back to riding *Theresa the Skateboard!* I felt so free! Had my mom known what I was doing she would have flipped out; so, we just sent her a picture.

I didn't realize how sick I felt because of my arm and the cancer until I didn't have it anymore. I felt like I could do anything, and I did! I was back to all of my regular activities and felt so alive and grateful!

When I got home from my surgery everyone wanted to congratulate me and gave me pats on the back or shoulder; they never knew, but it was stabbingly painful. My family had to tell people at church not touch me because it was so bad. I even got a sign that I wore saying, "Don't hug or touch". I loved them all dearly and I never pushed anyone away or said that I was in pain, I just sucked it up. When I would get home, I would totally crash and have to recharge again.

I didn't see myself as having a disability, it was just the new and improved me! Physically I felt great, as long as my back or shoulders weren't bumped. That caused quite a bit of pain. I used several pain medications to keep it under control. I was feeling phantom arm pains, it was so crazy. It felt like it was still there, but it wasn't.

Weeks after I got home from my surgery the scouts were planning to leave for the Klondike Derby winter camp. I wasn't about that miss that! So, I got all packed up, got together a bag of morphine and Mom dropped me off to the scoutmaster. He was mortified. I still had my staples and stitches and I was about to go to an overnight winter camp where we would be making snow caves to sleep in all night long. I had a blast! I was only five merit badges away from achieving my

Eagle Scout award.

As with any cancer treatment or major surgery like that, I had to be constantly monitored to make sure my body was functioning with the medications and healing properly. In March I went in for a checkup. The doctor told me that the cancer had spread. The tumor had grown into my right shoulder. I also had three spots on my lungs and lymph nodes. I didn't have long to live; they estimated six months. I was extremely upset and emotional. I just wanted to be a kid. I decided that I was in God's hands now and that I was going to live every breath of the rest of my life full of purpose and joy.

With my father in the air force, we had some amazing contacts. A friend showed us enormous amounts of generosity and love and helped me to get the care I needed. I am forever honored and grateful for those individuals. You know who you are.

I made a bucket list and excitedly started achieving things I'd always dreamed of doing. It was such a blast! I had promised my girlfriend that I would take her to the prom. With a lot of painkillers, and some firm self-talk and mental stamina, I was able to dance and be around that massive crowd of teenagers being touched, loved and supported. I have such dear friends and hope they know how truly wonderful they were at supporting me through my earthly trial. It was always important to me that others were lifted up no matter what.

I was racing to enjoy life. I did things for the joy of doing things; like beating my grandpa at chess. I wanted to do things big, have fun, but most importantly I wanted to do things for other people. I had the opportunity to go to Disney World for two weeks. My brother and sister were working there for a time. When I saw children there in wheelchairs with the Make-a-Wish Foundation, I would always go up to talk to them. I'd give them courage and show them my battle scars of courage. I wanted them to know that I was just like them; fighting cancer and now I'm home having fun, and they could be too.

I would play full out, doing everything to the max. I had a crazy goal to hunt and shoot a wild turkey. When we got to the farm they were running everywhere, between all the corn stalks. We finally cornered one, then I realized with one arm I couldn't hold the rifle by myself to shoot it. So, I improvised! I asked my friend to kneel down so I could use his shoulder to put my gun against while I aimed and shot a 26-pound turkey!

I continued to ride my beloved *Theresa the Skateboard* until I couldn't stand up anymore. I felt as though my spirit was taking over my body – I had no more strength. It was an interesting process and transition to know that I was slowly dying. I felt and spoke with more maturity than a 16-year-old kid. I was always noticing miracles and talking to my parents about them.

I am beyond grateful for my family, friends and loved ones who were a part of my journey on earth. Your support, however small, has not gone unnoticed and it's important that you know how greatly loved and grateful I am that you were a part of my life. Till we meet again.

MY NAME IS JEFFERY.
I had BONE CANCER and an AMPUTATED ARM.
What's YOUR Superpower?

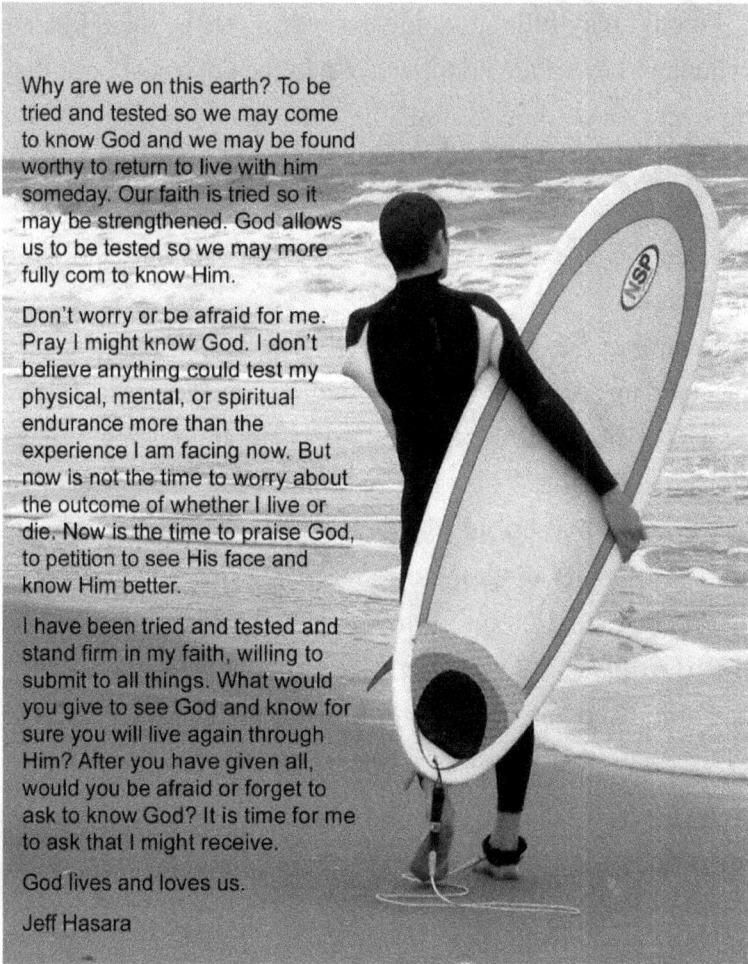

Why are we on this earth? To be tried and tested so we may come to know God and we may be found worthy to return to live with him someday. Our faith is tried so it may be strengthened. God allows us to be tested so we may more fully com to know Him.

Don't worry or be afraid for me. Pray I might know God. I don't believe anything could test my physical, mental, or spiritual endurance more than the experience I am facing now. But now is not the time to worry about the outcome of whether I live or die. Now is the time to praise God, to petition to see His face and know Him better.

I have been tried and tested and stand firm in my faith, willing to submit to all things. What would you give to see God and know for sure you will live again through Him? After you have given all, would you be afraid or forget to ask to know God? It is time for me to ask that I might receive.

God lives and loves us.

Jeff Hasara

Reviews Continued

"In reading this, I learned how valuable a skill it is to be able to relate to other people, by understanding how they approach their challenges. This book is important because it showcases everyone's own unique talents and abilities, and how they overcome challenges to live a full, enriching life. Reading these stories made me feel delighted; it's a heartwarming book with a powerful message. This book should be required reading for everyone – parents, students, and the world at large. It is an easy way to learn how other people overcome their challenges in their everyday lives."

Michelle Zoromski
Executive Director, Reece's Rainbow Down Syndrome Adoption Grant Foundation
WI, USA
www.ReecesRainbow.org

"I thoroughly enjoyed reading *What's YOUR Superpower? From Special Needs to Super Heroes*. I was hooked by the first story—especially with the strong personalities telling the stories—and I couldn't stop reading. Each story is heartfelt, beautiful, and truly inspiring. As a school librarian and former classroom teacher, I know the deep need for books like this to teach the importance of embracing differences and combatting bullying. As the mother of twin boys with special needs, the stories brought tears to my eyes over and over again as I pictured these stories motivating my boys when they're older. The stories prove that people are both incredible and resilient. They need to be told and retold. I'm ready for the sequel!"

Becca Ingersoll
School Librarian, Former English Teacher, Special Needs Mom
UT, USA

"We read this book to my children ages 7, 5 and 3. They loved hearing everyone's story and learning about other special people. We have a 9-month-old baby with a rare brain malformation and a rare form of epilepsy. This book helped our children to understand that it's okay that their brother is "special" in his own way."

LeiLani and Melvin Daly USVI
Mom of four superheroes,
Former CLA and airline stewardess
St Thomas US Virgin Islands

"This book has the power to change your life! I love how the stories are written from the perspective of the child or highlighted person. It gives you a glimpse into their world and viewing life from their lens. It made me realize that any disability is really a superpower waiting to be discovered, and it's all in how you perceive it."

Kash Bhatti
Pakastanian Former Banking Analyst
Financial Adviser with Managed Wealth Financial
www.managedwealthfinancial.com
SLC, UT, USA

"*What's YOUR Superpower*" has been such a joy to read with my husband and our five children (ages 2-11). We adopted two of our five children through foster care as special needs children. They too have surprising abilities! Each of our children do. This book helps us to see what our individual superpowers are and inspires us to be better. I love how eye- opening this book has been for our family as we read about so many different real-life experiences, challenges and accomplishments. We love the special messages shared. This book is very engaging for children and adults alike. Thank you, Marcy, for dedicating your life to such a great cause and for sharing such great insights with the world!

Michelle Trujillo
Mother to 5 awesome kiddos (some biological, some adopted)
CA, USA

"This is a powerful book! I genuinely believe that each person who reads it will come away with at least one new insight: greater compassion for others, more gratitude for their life, appreciation for their struggles, or a desire to serve those who have super powers that differ from their own. It's time to remove the awkwardness and embrace the humanity that unites us all as we love and serve each other."

Livia Pewtress
Creator, Author, Mentor, Wellness Advocate, Inspiration
UT, USA

"I enjoyed the fact that Marcy described the Superpowers in both technical and straightforward terms. Even with a background in the medical field, I found that I learned and better understood this aspect of life from reading this book. Marcy doesn't ask anything of you but to realize your own and others' superpowers. How many times has someone made your day with a smile, a laugh, or just giving you a really good hug? These individuals recognize that power of simplicity and happily share it with the world."

Kenneth W. Myers
Author
UT, USA

"I've always wanted a super power too, and Marcy has just introduced us to a host of real-life Super Heroes right here among us. With each introduction, you just want to jump into their amazing life and try on their super power. If only everyone could know the gifts and talents God has placed on each of us in the most beautiful and unique ways, wouldn't our world be just amazing!"

Robin Sizemore
Executive Director, Hopscotch Adoptions, Inc.
Armenia, Bulgaria, Georgia, Ghana, Guyana, Morocco, Serbia and Ukraine
Pre-& Post-Adoption Services available to NY and NC residents
Ph: 336.899.0068
www.hopscotchadoptions.org.

About the Author

Marcy Valenzuela is the wife to the man of her dreams, Robinson, and mother to 10 children. Five of her children were born with disabilities, seven are in heaven, and one is adopted. She and her husband are currently raising three young children who often get mistaken for 3-year-old triplets. Both of their daughters have down syndrome and their living son is their only child born with no disabilities.

Marcy is a dedicated mother, wife, and homemaker with a passion for making things beautiful and giving love wherever she goes. Anyone who knows her will tell you how highly optimistic, positive, and inspiring she is. She continually spreads happiness and joy despite the trials she has faced. She's got an incredible outlook on life. She is courageous and has a fierce determination to achieve her goals.

Were it not for her 110% diligence, her daughter, Sofia, would never have come to her family, an adoption which was 100% fund-raised. After returning from the many orphanages she and her husband visited in Armenia she wished she could have adopted them all. Then a realization and voice came to her saying, "It's not your job to adopt them all, it's your job to find their parents."

This is the first book of several in an attempt to inspire, educate, and light a fire within families to consider adoption... even to a child who may have special needs. Marcy is an advocate of special needs children of all ages and wishes to educate, lift, and encourage others to know that we are all God's children. We all need love and acceptance.

Her own children have brought happiness, joy, goodness, and blessings to her family; blessings that can happen in no other way than to love and raise a child with special needs. There is so much to celebrate with these children, and Marcy's dream is to help families not only to decide to adopt a child, whether the child is typically developing or otherwise, but to take fast action and RUN to that child. It's time to get these children out of the abuse and neglect they are currently in and bring them home to a loving family.

Don't walk – RUN.

www.WhatsYourSuperpowerBooks.com

www.ingramcontent.com/pod-product-compliance
Lightning Source LLC
Chambersburg PA
CBHW070812280326
41934CB00012B/3166